My Little Book of

River Otters

By Hope Irvin Marston
Illustrated by Maria Magdalena Brown

NorthWord Press

Minnetonka, Minnesota
www.howtobookstore.com

The chubby river otter snuggled into her cozy bed of leaves and moss in an old beaver den. Outside, snow blanketed the ground.

The next morning her three little cubs were born. They were about the size of baby kittens.

The mother otter nuzzled her babies to her belly to nurse.

The cubs ate until their tummies were full.

Swish! Swish! Swish! Swish! Swish!

The mother otter washed each baby with her tongue.
The otters cuddled together and slept.

Their mother curled around them and kept them warm.

Their father brought a fish to eat near the den, but he didn't come in yet.

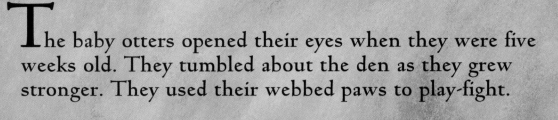

The baby otters opened their eyes when they were five weeks old. They tumbled about the den as they grew stronger. They used their webbed paws to play-fight.

Their mother patted them and rolled them over in play.

One spring day the mother otter led her babies to the opening of the den.

"Chirp—chirp—chirp," she called.

They followed her on wobbly legs.

Suddenly, down
the hill they tumbled!

Their thick fur kept
them from getting hurt.

The otter nudged her babies toward the river with her little black nose. She slipped into the water.

She called to the babies.
But they were afraid to go to her.

The otter swam back to shore. She grabbed one little cub by the scruff of the neck.

Splash! She dropped him into the water.

Up he bobbed to the surface. His fluffy coat helped him float.

The mother otter turned back to the river bank.
The other babies climbed onto her back.

Down she dived into the water.

Up popped the babies!

They began to swim on their own.

The parents dived to the bottom of the river. The babies watched them use their paws and whiskers to search for something to eat.

The mother otter caught a fish and carried it to shore in her mouth.

She gave it to her hungry babies. Then she dived back into the water to catch another fish.

By the time they were four months old, the otters were catching their own fish. And frogs and tadpoles and little turtles.

They dived to the bottom of the river and wiggled their whiskers under rocks, feeling for crayfish.

Day after day they swam in the river.
They dived. They played.

They glided along on their stomachs.
Then they flipped on their backs and floated.
They played follow-the-leader.

Their mother played with them all summer.

Their father played with the cubs too.

His whiskers twitched and he called to them.

"Un! Un! Un!"

The young otters chased after him. Their mother joined the race.

Along the river bank and into the water.

Out of the water.

And back in again!

The father otter ran and slid on a grassy field. The cubs watched.

Run-and-slide. Run-and-slide. Run-and-slide.

What fun! Soon the whole otter family was sliding across the grass.

The next day it rained.

SWOOOOOOOOSH!

The otters glided down the slippery mud into the river.

One autumn day, one of the young otters found a pretty stone on the river bottom. She swam to the surface with the stone. She flipped on her back and juggled it in her paws.

Then she hid it in the river bank so she could play with it later.

When winter returned, snow again blanketed the ground. The otter family had fun sliding down snow-covered hills.

The father dived into a snow bank and dug underneath it with his short legs. The others poked their noses into the snow looking for him.

Surprise!

He popped up right under their noses.

Then the river turned to ice.

The otters didn't mind. They liked sliding on the ice . . . and swimming below it.

Tiny pads on their hind feet kept them from slipping when they walked. Tufts of hair between their toes kept their feet warm.

When they tired,
they scooted into their den.

The otter family breathed
from air pockets under the ice.
Or at breathing holes in the ice.

They fished for suckers and sunfish.

They dug up frogs and insect larvae.

When spring came, the young otters moved out of the family den to make room for new babies.

But they stayed close by
to welcome their new
brothers and sisters.

DEDICATION
For Bryan and Elizabeth

The author wishes to thank Mr. Ed Spevak, Assistant Curator of Mammals,
Bronx Zoo for his kind assistance and advice.

© Hope Irvin Marston, 1998
Illustrations © Maria Magdalena Brown, 1998

NorthWord Press
5900 Green Oak Drive
Minnetonka, MN 55343
1-800-328-3895
www.howtobookstore.com

Book design by Russell S. Kuepper

Library of Congress Cataloging-in-Publication Data
Marston, Hope Irvin.
    My little book of river otters / by Hope Irvin Marston:
illustrations by Maria Magdalena Brown.
        p.   cm.
    Summary: A pair of river otters care for their young and watch them
grow and learn.
    ISBN 1-55971-639-8 (pbk)
        1. Otters--Juvenile fiction. [1. Otters--Fiction.]
    I. Brown, Maria Magdalena, ill. II. Title.
PZ10.3.M3545Mt 1998
[Fic] -- dc21   97-5958

Printed in Malaysia
10 9 8 7 6 5 4 3 2